In the Name of Allah (swt), the Kind, the Merciful

Published by Sun Behind the Cloud Publications Ltd
PO Box 15889, Birmingham, B16 6NZ
This edition first published in 2022
Copyright © Zainab A and Sun Behind the Cloud 2022
Illustrations by Michael Barnes
The moral rights of the authors have been asserted
All rights reserved
A CIP catalogue record for this book is available from the British Library
Printed in Turkey by Mega Printing

ISBN (print): 978-1-908110-82-4
www.sunbehindthecloud.com
info@sunbehindthecloud.com

The humorous stories of Bahlool as told and re-told by madrasah teachers and speakers for generations have given us a glimpse of what it means to be a loyal companion of an Imam.

Bahlool lived at the time of Imam Ja'far as Sadiq (as) and Imam Musa al-Kadhim (as). The fear of persecution at the hands of the Abbasid Caliphs forced the followers of the Ahlulbayt to look to creative ways to preserve their lives while continuing to support the mission of Islam and maintaining it's true sanctity. Bahlool adopted the life of insanity to save his life and serve Islam at the advice of the Imam. All the while imparting valuable lessons to those around him as well as the Caliph himself!

This book attempts to bring some of those stories to life in a way that children can relate to. It was inspired by a little child's love for poetry and the need to offer the children in our community a fun book of rhymes that imparts valuable gems found within our faith.

The amazing contributions of fallible companions of the Aimmah show us the amazing potential Allah has given to each and every one of us. It is my prayer that this book invites our children to build a bond with the amazing personality of Bahlool. May our families be blessed with some of his unflinching loyalty and servitude to the Imam of his time (AJTF).

My heartfelt appreciation to my family for their faith and encouragement as we worked to bring this vision to reality. I am deeply grateful for the opportunity to work with Sun Behind The Cloud Publications who spent countless hours bringing this work to fruition in it's fullest potential.

-Zainab A.

# Contents

The Price of Good Advice...................P6

Neighbour Danger............................P16

What's in a Name?..........................P32

- The Price of Paradise..........................P38
- Seating for a Beating!.....................P48
- What's a Kingdom worth?..................P56
- A Great Debate............................P66

# The Price of Good Advice

A man came from Baghdad one day,
Looking for good business advice.
He decided to ask a special man,
They called Bahlool 'The Wise'

"Salaam, O Shaykh," he said to him,
"I'm desperate for success,
But everything I've tried so far,
Has ended in a mess!"

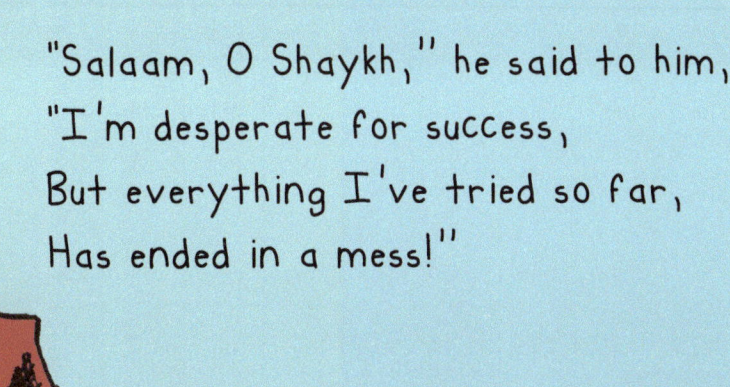

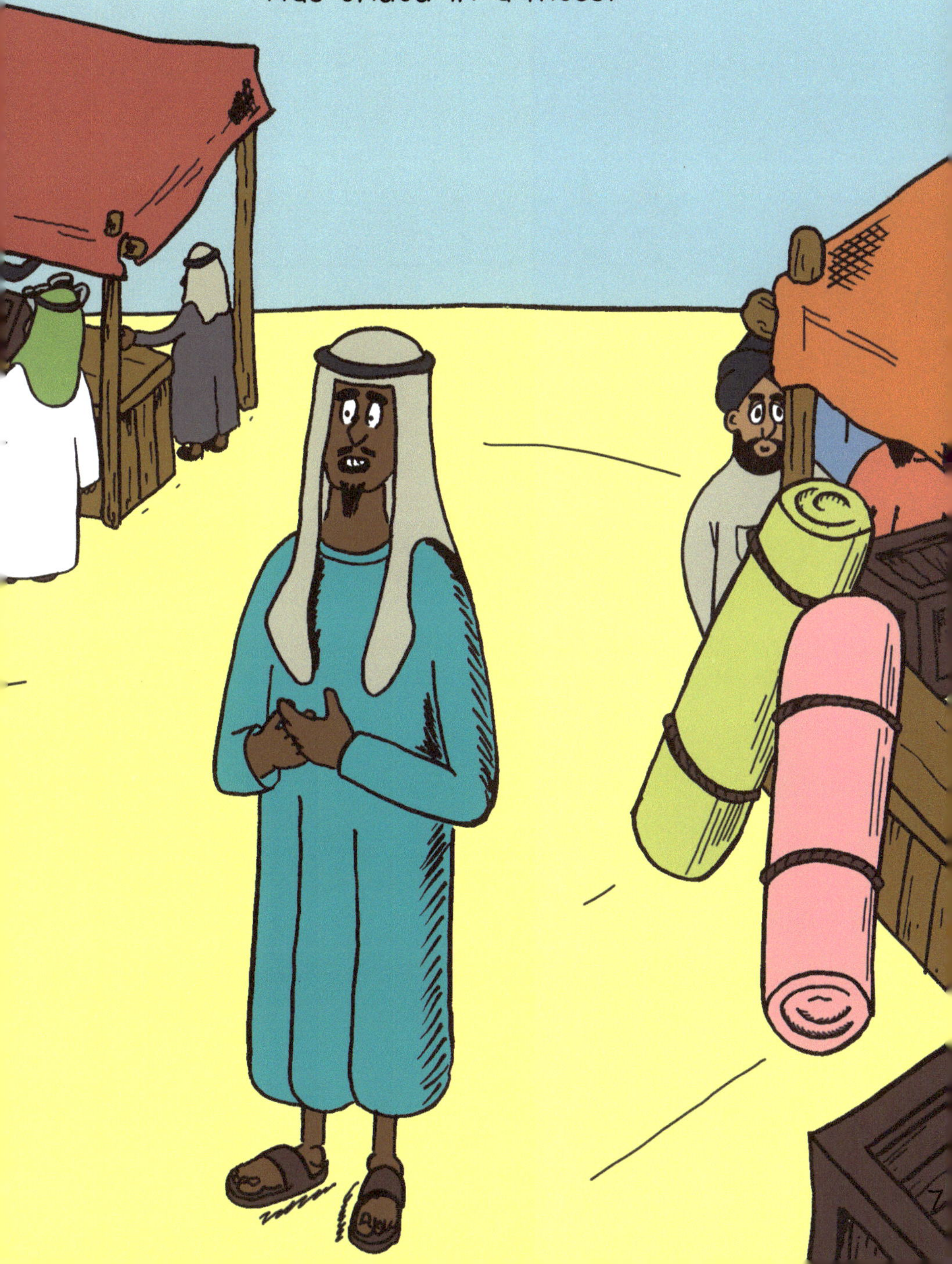

"Peace be on you," replied Bahlool,
"Pray tell me what you need
I'll help you in any way I can,
And God-Willing you will succeed!"

"What should I buy, O Shaykh," he asked
"That will be good to sell?"
"Cotton" replied Bahlool "and Iron too,
Both will serve you well."

So the man took Bahlool's advice,
And made lots and lots of money
Then - as a rich man - he returned to ask,
But this time from Bahlool 'The Funny'

"Funny Crazy Bahlool!" he began to mock,
"I am here to pick your brain,
What should I buy, that will yield profits high,
And earn me lots again?"

Bahlool gave the man a long, hard look,
Then he replied in a firm voice,
"Buy onions," he said, "and melons as well,
These should next be your choice."

The man hurried away happily
But what do you think happened next?
He was soon back in the city of Baghdad,
Bothered, flustered and vexed!

"It all rotted!" he cried, "All my money is lost!
I thought you were clever and wise!
But the advice you gave me was totally worthless,
You're just a fool in disguise!"

Bahlool smiled at the angry man,
"Calm down," he said, "no need to shout,
If you will let me speak, I'll tell you why
you have nothing to complain about."

"When first you came, you asked from a Shaykh,
You were not interested in fooling around,
You presented your sincere request,
So the advice you got was sound."

"The second time you called someone else
You asked a funny, crazy man what he thought.
So that time I only told you
What a funny, crazy man would have bought!"

The man looked away, red-faced with shame,
He had learnt the Bahlool way
To choose with care the way he spoke
And the words he chose to say.

# Neighbour Danger

Times were hard and Bahlool took care
To save whatever he could,
When he happened to earn a few gold coins,
He would bury them — as a wise man should.

One afternoon, his pockets were full,
After working hard all day,
He had enough to feed himself,
And even give some money away.

When he got back home, he took his gold
And straight into his garden he went
With a simple plan which was...
To hide what he hadn't spent.

His only neighbour – a cobbler
(who lived across the street)
Happened to be at the window
And saw this secret retreat!

"Ah Bahlool!" he said to himself, his eyes widening with pleasure, "you really should be more careful, About where you keep your treasure!"

Not long after, one quiet day
When Bahlool was not about
The cobbler grabbed at his chance
And dug the treasure out!

"Finders, keepers!" the shoemaker thought
as he sneaked it out of sight
"If you don't want to lose your gold,
Then don't hide it in broad daylight!"

When Bahlool next went to his spot,
To find the extra cash,
He dug the hole to find
There was nothing in his stash!

Bahlool was astonished to learn
He'd lost the fruit of all his labour
He knew straight away who was to blame,
And marched across to visit his neighbour.

"Salaam!" He called out loudly
His voice was filled with cheer,
"Salaam to you too...wweelcome in,"
the neighbour replied with fear.

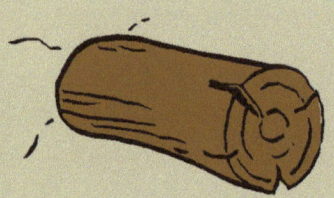

When he entered the neighbour's house,
Bahlool didn't accuse or blame,
Instead, he had a trick up his sleeve
That would bring the cobbler to shame.

"I have a problem," Bahlool said,
"And you seem a clever man,
I'd take the advice you give because
You seem to know how to plan."

"You see, I've buried wealth across the town –
In places here and there.
But it's getting harder to keep track of it all...
I don't have the time to spare."

As they spoke, he told the cobbler
Of more money he had to hide,
"Should I bury it all in one place?" he asked
"and put them side by side?"

"Of course," the cobbler nodded
"And yes, you're very right
You need to save both time and space,
It makes sense to have ONE site!"

To himself he thought, "How clever of me!
What a golden chance this seems!
Once Bahlool does what I suggest,
"I'll be wealthy beyond my dreams!"


He'd have to put back what he'd stolen,
And do it pretty fast
But in its stead he thought he'd get
riches that were vast.

That very night, the cobbler returned
The money he had taken,
He thought that he could fool Bahlool,
But he was truly mistaken!

Bright and early the next morning,
Bahlool packed without hesitation
He dug up all his gold
And then moved to a new location!

The cobbler waited by his window
To see when Bahlool would return,
But when the night began to fall
He started to feel concern.

Had Bahlool really left?
And taken his riches too?
He needed to learn a lesson from this,
And act like a neighbour should do!

Fazl asked Bahlool, "What should I call this jewel?
What name should I inscribe on the door?"
Bahlool thought hard and asked him,
"Who was this mosque built for?"

"For Allah alone!" Fazl cried.
"There's no shadow of a doubt
This has been my lifelong quest
That's why I've gone all out!"

# BY BAHLOOL

Bahlool looked up at the ornate door
"If what you say is really true,
Then please write my name there,
It should make no difference to you!"

"But I built it!" Fazl gasped in shock,
"It was MY hard work and MY money.
If there's a name up there, it should be mine
Don't make jokes like that, it's not funny!"

"That's exactly the point, my dear man,
The name on the door shouldn't matter.
When we dedicate acts only to Allah,
It shouldn't be for people to flatter."

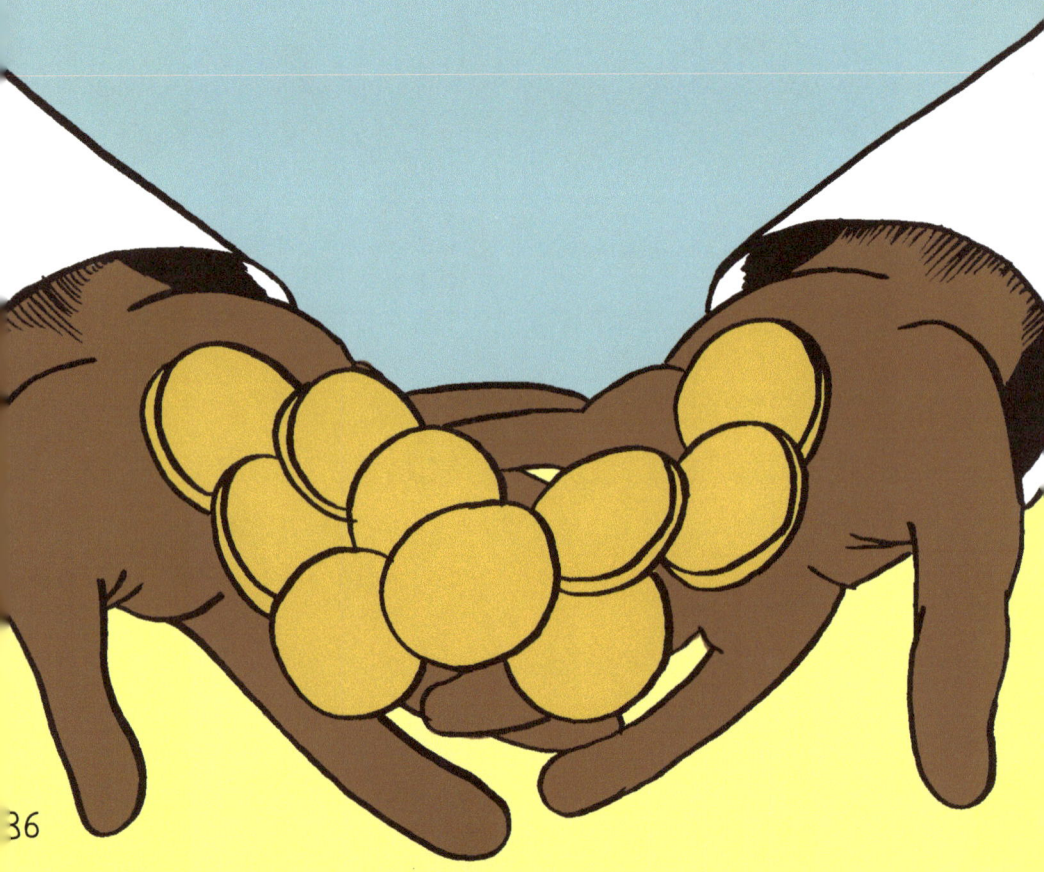

# The Price of Paradise!

The wife of a greedy king,
Was a queen who was very smart.
She was also a kind and gentle soul,
Who loved Allah with all her heart!

She used to go around the city,
To see how people were faring,
And figure out how to help them,
For it was her nature to be caring.

She ventured one day to the river,
With her entourage making her way.
When she stumbled upon Bahlool,
Building gardens out of clay.

"What are you doing?" she asked kindly,
Admiring his childish art,
"Busy making Jannah for those,
Who want an early start!"

"How much for one?" she inquired.
He offered it for a hundred dinar,
"It's a deal" she said, handing over the coins.
To those watching it seemed bizarre!

Bahlool distributed the money
Amongst the poor and needy.
He wasn't keen on worldly riches,
And he certainly wasn't greedy!

That night as the King's wife slept,
She dreamt of a place like no other,
With flowers and fruits and favours,
One blessing on top of another!

There were high palaces of jewels,
Winding rivers of refreshing drink,
A scroll was handed to her with
"From Bahlool" written in golden ink.

She woke up thrilled and rushed
to narrate her dream to the King,
"A hundred dinar?" he asked puzzled,
"For a garden in Jannah? That's nothing!"

The next morning, he summoned Bahlool
And demanded a garden of his own,
"I'm not selling any more," Bahlool replied
"Why not?!" he began to moan.

The King continued his outburst
He too wanted a heavenly place
Bahlool laughed "Don't be such a child,
You've not quite understood the case."

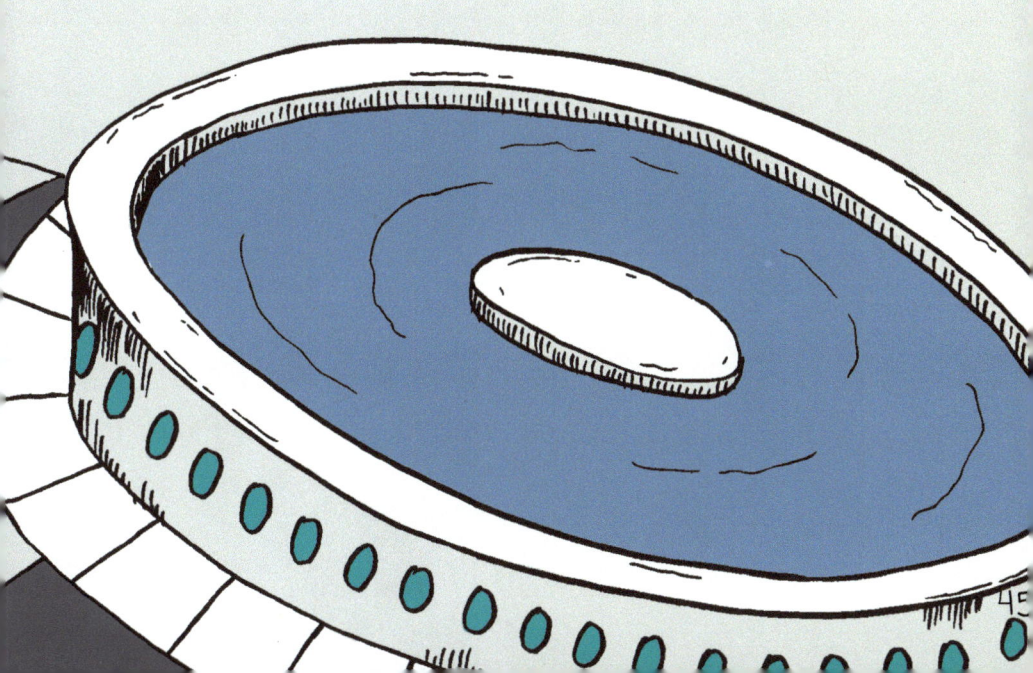

"Your wife bought the garden from me
Out of the kindness of her heart.
It wasn't a transaction for a reward,
Do you see the lesson I'm trying to impart?"

"You on the other hand
Want to grab a piece of land
Even though you've done nothing
To earn it by your hand."

"I advise you to learn from your wife
And be good for Allah's sake
That is what you will need to do
If it's a garden you want to make."

# Seating for a beating

It happened every so often
That the King felt tired or drained
And so he would call for Bahlool,
Sure to be entertained.

On one such occasion,
Bahlool was early to report
He found the King had not arrived
And he was alone in the court

The courtroom was extremely lavish
Every detail proper and prim
The pillars were made of marble
And every seat had a golden trim!

In the middle of the room stood a throne,
Its seat empty and inviting.
Bahlool sat down on its cushion,
Can you imagine what happened to him?

The guards caught sight of Bahlool,
Sitting where he shouldn't be.
They ran in and rushed to grab him,
And tied him so he couldn't get free!

Bahlool was beaten and bruised
For something he shouldn't have done.
Who would have thought sitting on a throne
Would be more than a bit of fun?

The King heard the commotion,
And quickly came to help
"What is going on? Stop this at once!"
"Leave him alone!" he yelped

The King gave Bahlool a curious glance
"Why did you sit on my throne?
Surely, even you must know
It is for me alone!"

"But come on now, no need to weep,
I've saved you from my men
I called you to entertain me
Let's now all smile again."

Bahlool replied, "It is not for me that I cry!
I am worried about you.
I only sat on a throne that I shouldn't
For less than a minute or two..."

"You've been sitting there for much longer
Even though it doesn't belong to you.
When Allah asks His questions
What ever will you do?"

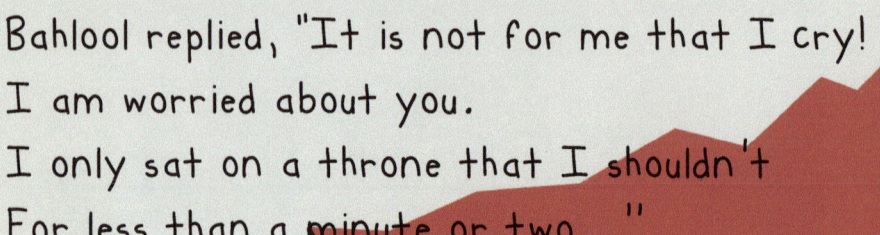

So, think about where you sit
And whether you deserve to be there.
Because nobody wants a beating
For not doing what is fair!

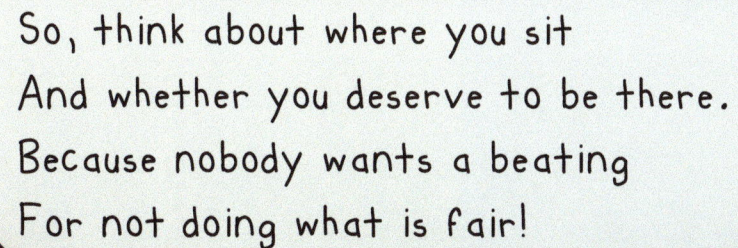

# What's a Kingdom Worth?

It was summer in the desert
With scorching blue skies
When the King told his messenger
To summon Bahlool the Wise.

The King was hot and bothered
And was tired of the day
"Bahlool, I'm interested to hear
In what you might have to say?"

"Do you have some advice for me?
Something I can think about?"
Bahlool knew what to say
Without a shadow of a doubt!

"Imagine yourself in the desert,
On a dry, sweltering day
You're thirsty and alone,
And have totally lost your way."

"What would you give to someone
If he came to you in that state,
With a cup of refreshing water,
To save you from your fate?"

"Gold dinars!" replied the King,
His chest puffed out with pride.
Bahlool smiled and asked him,
"What if that offer was denied?"

The King paused to think,
What would he pay to live?
"Half of my kingdom," he said
"That's what I'd happily give!"

Bahlool had another question
For the eager, boastful king.
"And what if your body could not get rid
of the water you were drinking?"

"What would you give for a cure
to the problem you'd then face?"
The King thought long and hard
About how he'd handle such disgrace.

"I would offer the other half of my kingdom"
He answered finally.
Bahlool looked at the king
Who was now sitting silently.

"You've said yourself, a cup of water
Is all your kingdom is worth.
Then why not change the way you behave
and tread humbly on the Earth?"

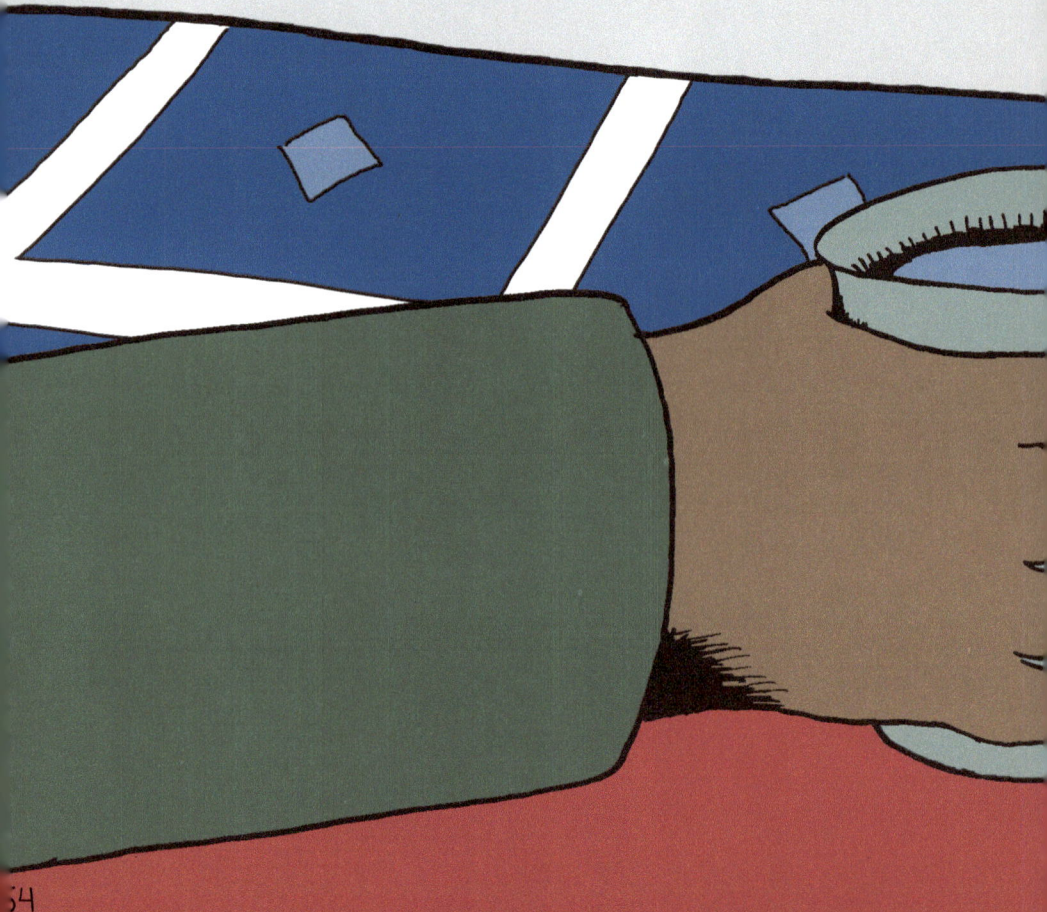

Treat others with kindness and justice
Your wealth alone cannot save you.
Remember only Allah is Needless
So beware of what you do.

# A Great Debate!

"I am an important man," began the Sheikh,
"Here to say, I disagree
About Ja'far as-Sadiq's conclusions
Which now amount to three."

"First, he talked about Shaytan,
Saying he will burn in hellfire.
But that's impossible because
How can fire burn fire?"

"Second, he says Allah can't be seen,
That can't be true I persist,
For we must be able to see something
To be able to say it exists!"

"The third conclusion I don't understand
Is that we're responsible for all we do.
But we couldn't do anything at all,
Unless Allah allowed us to!"

Luckily Bahlool was standing nearby,
and he had an amazing plan
He picked up a rock and to everyone's shock,
Threw it straight at the astonished man!

Bahlool was arrested and taken straight to the judge
To explain what he had done.
Of course, Bahlool had an answer for everything,
He didn't just throw it for fun!

The Sheikh stood rubbing his head
And complained that it really hurt.
Bahlool innocently asked, "How can this be?
Aren't we all made from dirt?"

"Of course Shaytan can burn in hellfire,
If you were hurt by clay.
Objects can be similar, yet different
That's what I'm trying to say."

The Sheikh, now angry, said
"Don't make excuses! I am obviously in pain!"
"But why arrest me?" Bahlool replied,
"Surely, I'm not to blame!"

"Didn't you say that Allah is the One
Who allows us to do what we do?
So why are you blaming me
If you believe your words to be true?"

"And anyway, didn't you say
That things have to be seen to exist?
Please show me then, so I too can see
This pain about which you insist."

Bahlool continued, "We are always responsible
For the way we act and behave.
Allah gives us freedom to choose right from wrong,
And then we will answer to Him in our grave."

"And there are so many things that we cannot see
That we believe are truly there.
Angels, jinn and past prophets,
Even the oxygen we breathe in the air!"

The Sheikh looked away, embarrassed
Then shamefaced, he left without a retort
He knew Ja'far as-Sadiq had been right,
And his arguments had fallen short!

# Did you enjoy this book?

Why not find out how you can use this book for theatrical productions and drama based activities for all ages.

Visit www.sunbehindthecloud.com or email us on info@sunbehindthecloud.com

www.ingramcontent.com/pod-product-compliance
Lightning Source LLC
Chambersburg PA
CBHW041605220426
43661CB00015B/1192